"An Everlasting Love"

My Father's Poetry

Author,
Albino H. González
Montesinos

Literary Work Published by
Rina A. González

"An Everlasting Love"

My Father's Poetry

Author, Albino H. González Montesinos

Literary Work Published by
Rina A. González

ISBN # **978**-0-9792408-7-4

Artistic Credits:

Collaborator ~ Flora González de Núñez
Translation, Cover and Interior Design
~ Rina A González

Flora & I

Index

Flora & Manny

Dedication

If my father was alive today, know that he would dedicate this book to his beloved wife, his 5 children, 18 grandchildren, 29 great-grandchildren, and his 3 great-great-grandchildren.

Through the publication of this book, it is my intent to give the reader and inside look to the dreams and aspirations of this profound being. As his decedents, we enjoy having his nobility, his love and his gift of laugher as well as many of his artistic abilities.

Although his literary work is incomplete, thought that keeping it to ourselves is selfish. Our mother 'Mima' kept them as her treasured memory, perhaps as evidence of their 'everlasting love'. As I read them again, after so many years came to understand that what you are holding in your hands is indeed 'my parents love story'.

We, their children, arc the heirs to their legacy, and dedicate this book to their brilliance, laughter, genius and to their indomitable spirit imbedded in our personalities.

May your spirit rejoice reading my father work. And as you become a witness to an undying love, you will have an inside look as to why his family keeps the memory alive.

With love,

Rina

The González-García Family
Photo taken by Pipo, January 1954,
San Miguel, El Sevillano, Havana, Cuba
Margarita's 1ˢᵗ birthday

Published by Rina A González

Prologue

This book contains the short literary work of my father, Albino H. González Montesinos. During one of the most emotional charged periods in his life, he was forced to take the decision of leaving his beloved family and country behind travelling to New York, where he quickly opened his own business as a designer and sculptor of fine jewelry in the Diamond District in the Metropolis of Manhattan.

The loneliness and nostalgia of his first winter in New York, separated from his wife, five children and his beloved Cuba, met the necessary condition needed for him to mold and sculpt words into rhymes.

It is also befitting that through the publication of his work, we, the daughters of Albino II. González Montesinos and his wife, Rina A. García de León, González, pay tribute to our parents loving memory. In life, we had the privilege of calling these two wonderful souls 'Pipo and Mima'. Today we want to thank them for how much they loved each other and for how much they loved their 5 children.

As daughter of this talented and noble man, I am proud to be the one to publish his literary work. My father was a passionate man and as such was a lover of beauty. His love, dedication, and abilities for the arts were unsurpassed. Today see that his family legacy is alive within each one of those he loved as well as in those he never met.

Pipo was a kind, loving, considerate, brilliant, and funny man. He was an exemplary son and brother, a good and generous friend, a loving and gentle soul who never forgot that laughter is the best medicine. He dedicated his live to loving everything and everyone. He made the best of things, even the bad times. To him every moment was an occasion to be happy, even if inside his heart was coming to pieces.

Yet, what I admire most about this unforgettable man is the deep love he had for his wife, our mother.

My wish is that as you read his work, come to feel the energy of love that comes through these pages. Moreover, as his passion emerges, you come to understand the powerful energy that has inspired his decedents to continue dreaming, creating, and loving life.

Sincerely, his daughter,

Rina A. González

Published by Rina A González

Published by Rina A González

The five children of Mima & Pipo {ages 14 -3}
Graduation of June 1956, Havana Cuba.
Days before our arrival in New York.

Published by Rina A González

To My Children

Havana, September 20, 1955

With Flora, Rina and Manuel
I want to add to my muse
The fragrance of wild flowers
That sprung from natures brew.

Without Rosa or Margarita
No verse could ever rhyme,
For they are the tender petals
That my heart dwells upon.

For my young and dear children
I give you my heart and soul,
And ask you to please forgive
The child inside this man.

Published by Rina A González

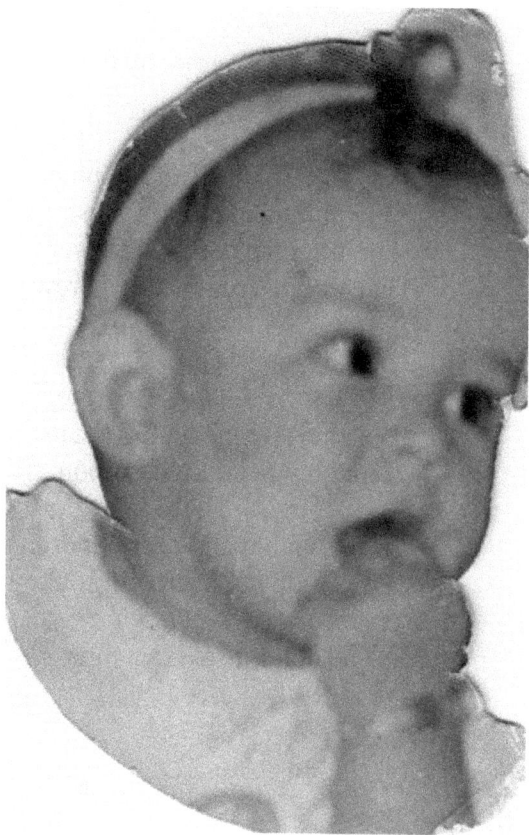

Margarita

Published by Rina A González

Margarita

Habana, September 20, 1955

Margarita, beautiful flower that inspires
The clean waters of my youth.
You will win much accolades
With your kind and gentle touch.

At all times your laughter's echoes
Throughout the house, so it seems.
And like your sisters enjoy
Having thoughts of what's to be.

Here is your older bother
That can help you in my stead.
So when you become a woman
Your laughter will never fade.

Published by Rina A González

Cuba's Flag and Code of Arms

Published by Rina A González

To My Homeland

Havana, September 20, 1955

I dedicate my humble verses
To my adored homeland,
With the faith of that great patriot
Who in vain gave to the lot.

Today I give you my verses
Which come from my very soul.
They are full of my compassion
For my homeland; my sweet home.

I share the fate of many
Who want to live a full life.
But not if to live my life
My homeland's liberty is in peril.

For what matters if her beauty
The clouds cover in their path.
When through my window can see
Happiness entering my heart.

Wild flowers grow in the mountain
Adorning the Great White River.
Peace will reign in my dear country
When impure hands are cleaner.

 Published by Rina A González

Empire State Building, N.Y.C.

Published by Rina A González

New York and I

Queens, New York, January 8, 1956

I

North, your mornings are cold,
And your nights are heavy, dreary.
Yet, colder than are your mornings
Are my eyes that longs to see them.

II

Two months with eight days have passed
The road is thick, dark, and dismal.
I ask the Almighty God
To make my days warn and cheerful.

III

The days become long and hard
When agony is your keeper.
Leaving my family behind
Is cruel, unjust; it's a gripper.

IV

North, let me dream again
With my children, and my wife;
So that happiness becomes
The echoing sound in my life.

Published by Rina A González

V

Without them, there is no joy
And there is pain in my life;
I am a father whose full trust
Is in the kindness of your heart.

VI

If you believe I can live
Without my family's embrace,
You have become as your mornings,
Cold and empty ~ shallow, grey.

VII

Christmas, toys, things, have just passed,
Yet, here I am, without them.
And in your mornings and nights
I feel the chill of my madness.

VIII

That is why North, I implore
That in your hospitable land,
You extent a helping hand
By answering this father's query.

Published by Rina A González

VIII

I give thanks to the Almighty
For appeasing my concerns
For I know that one day soon
They will come and end my pain.

IX

I want to thank my sweet children
And the woman I adore,
For giving peace to this man,
And a heart that longs to hold you, for evermore.

With love; to my children and wife.

    Published by Rina A González

Rosa

To My Rosa

Queens, New York   February 14, 1956

In thinking that I'm a poet,
You have placed me in a jam;
But I will try to deliver
Since you have given me the change.

Today I will rhyme for Rosa,
As if a poet I was.
What a cute and funny girl;
Whose mumps have already passed.

I am thankful for the wisdom,
That you have shown me dear Rosa
For allowing my inspiration
To create a poem for you.

Now I have a request,
For you and your dear mother;
Take care of Margarita;
That she doesn't get your mumps.

To my loving daughter, Rosa

   Published by Rina A González

Flora Montesinos Felipez de González
Our Paternal Grandmother

Published by Rina A González

Albino H. González Montesinos

I want to be like the wind

Queens, New York   February 14, 1956

I want to be like the wind
Flying above in the heavens;
Become a mystical being
Making our love last forever.

I want to experience infancy
By reverting to the womb.
And once there thus experience
How the flower turns to bloom.

I want to hear my mother,
Be attentive to her words.
As pure light emerges
From her face as if a bird.

Be like the waters in spring;
Ever happy, always moving.
I want to kiss my five children
Hold them tightly in the morning.

It is because of this yearning
That I've revert to my youth;
Man's most precious moment lost,
Gone forever; slowly turning into dust.

That is why I ask the wind
To take me back to my infancy,
Where I can be close to my children
Understanding life's delusions.

                    Published by Rina A González

I am reduced by the storm
Of my mind's cruelest illusion.
I want to be like the wind
And be free from all confusion.

Published by Rina A González

Feliscindo González Yglesias
Our Paternal Grandfather

  Published by Rina A González

Mima, walking through the streets of Havana

Published by Rina A González

My Plea

Queens, New York   February 15, 1956

What life is this?
Seeing the hours go by
And every tick of the clock
Reminding me of what I've missed.

Knowing that my entire family
Are without me, by themselves,
Causes great pain and discomfort;
I so long for their embrace.

That is why today I beg,
I implore. No! I plea,
That my family can come
So that my sorrow can cease.

At all times my dear God,
Your presence I feel within.
And ask that you look after them
In my absence, till we meet.

If man's struggles and suffering
Are meant to wipe away sin,
Then my life has found its freedom
From the torments of ill will.

                    Published by Rina A González

Yet, knowing that suffering comes
From the illusion of man,
I ask that you heal my sorrow
By lending a helping hand.

Allow this heart to enfold
Allow my hands to create;
Fill these empty arms of mine
With their sweet, tender embrace.

May I see them very soon.
May we find the joy we seek.
Reward us by answering this plea,
By giving us your heavenly bliss.

Remove all doubts, dear God.
Appease my thoughts; clear my senses.
Bring me the joy of my life,
To these arms forever, present.

With all my love, to my precious jewels.

Published by Rina A González

"Cuba "

Queens, New York, February 25, 1956

"Our Nation is altar not pedestal"
Jose Martí

Cuba, my dear Homeland
How much pain you've had to bear.
You have never been governed
With a just and virtuous flair.

Those courageous, glorious souls
Who in the past gave their lives
Fighting to gain your freedom,
Would call the acts of a few
Cowardly, insidious, delirious!

Yesterday, these brave young men
Gave their lives fighting the Spaniards.
Their blood fell onto the ground
As you claimed your rightful triumph.

Each man fought courageously
Through their valor, they did conquer.
Yet today find that greed
Is the food for hollow stomachs.

As you can see,
In the absence of dignity,
There cannot be any glory.
No one dares to proclaim
What is just or made of onyx.

Published by Rina A González

Today it's not an invader
Or a tyrant who afflict you.
The ones causing you cruel pain
Are your children; that's despicable.

Martí, who was our redeemer
And died because of his love
Died in Dos Rios one day
With his face towards the sun.

Maceo, the great gladiator
Made the steeple bell sound loudly.
He also died for your cause,
In Havana, as a token of his valor.

If the dead heroes could see
The pain that a few have caused,
From their graves they would return
To punish those without cause.

Why are those that govern
My dear country corrupt?
They take the will of the people
By turning honor into dust.

As I look around can't find
Honor in recent behavior.
Can't find the glimmer of hope
In the eyes and hearts of neighbors.

Published by Rina A González

The ruthless care not
If tomorrow ever comes.
They just think of taking all
That their arms and legs can carry.

It seems that we have become
A nation of horrid men.
As if our country could withstand
The sins of a loveless friend.

They don't believe in forgiveness
Or care how much Cuba suffers.
They are dragons that devour
Her treasures and her white roses.

Because of our lack of love
We see that peace has its price.
One day we will come to know
That forsake Cuba, we cannot!

In holding on to what is real
I call on the brave, bold souls
That will rescue our dear country
From the hands of those who lust.

I call upon everyone
In whose veins run moral fiber.
Let us stop the maddening crowd
By freeing our beloved country!

Three cheers for our beloved,
Cuba, the Island of Hope.
The beautiful, the magnificent.
The one graced by three white doves.

Published by Rina A González

Flora

Published by Rina A González

Prologue to Florita

Queens, New York   March 3, 1956

In eulogies and sympathy
From a daughter to her father,
You have asked me for a poem
Thinking that I have the talent.

Since I am your father
You having my very essence,
I will try to rhyme some words
That will bring peace to your senses.

Hope!

In the midst of my loneliness
I have the comfort of knowing
That I can place all my hopes
In the Lady of the White Veil.

Want you to know that in my room
I have a picture of all five.
I can feel your fragrance closer
As I gaze upon its sight.

As wise children you have noticed,
Have perceived that I'm saddened.
Know that what is causing the pain
In the absence of my family.

    Published by Rina A González

Faith gives me of its peace,
The heaven's opens its doors,
So that I can find the answer
In the bosom of my Mother.

The Lady of the White Veil
Vanishes all my discomforts.
By giving peace to your father
For soon, you'll be at my door.

With love to my daughter, Florita.

{The Lady of the White Veil mentioned in this poem is,
La Virgen de la Caridad Del Cobre,
The Patron Saint of Cuba}

Published by Rina A González

Picture of Mima and Pipo, pregnant of Flora

Published by Rina A González

*Mima with Flora in arms, holding our cousins
Leonor by the hand, pregnant of me.*

Published by Rina A González

Mima pregnant of Manny walking with Flora and me.

Published by Rina A González

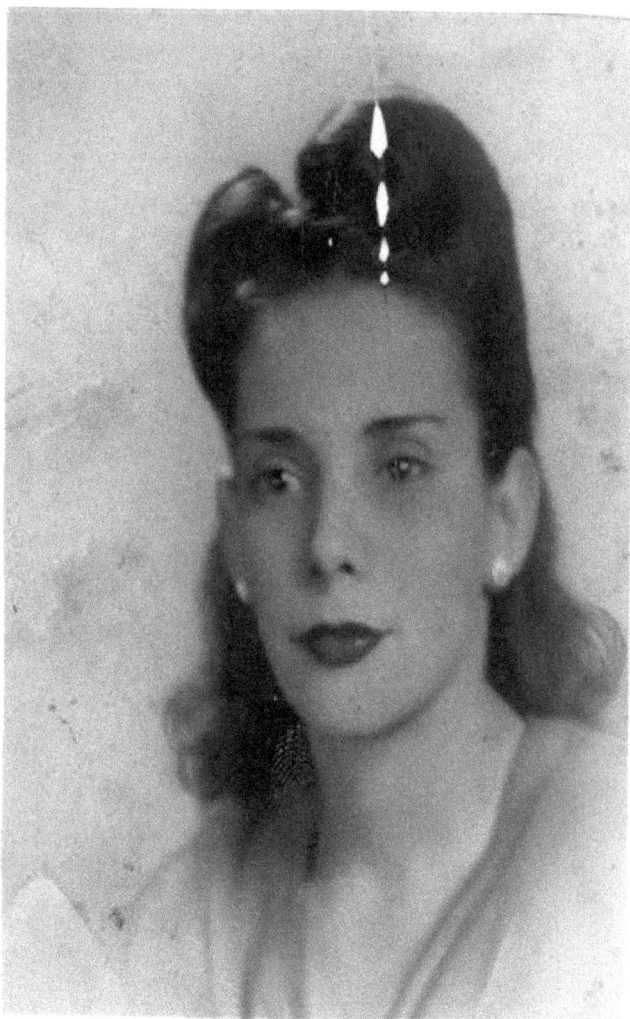

Rina A. García de León

Published by Rina A González

An Everlasting Love

Queens, New York   March 3, 1956

From the day when I first met you
And saw you for the first time,
I must admit that my soul,
Went after your loving heart.

Today, as I recall that moment
Do remember how I trembled.
Yet, my heart knew it had found
Love when at first I met you.

To add more joy to our love,
You have blessed me with five children;
Four girls and one boy,
Who add such pride to our prism.

Of our love, they are the flowers,
To love and nourish through life.
Without you, I would be nothing
You'd be the love to be found.

You're my everlasting love.
You are the owner of my heart.
You are the sun and you're the moon.
Forever, you will be mine.

   Published by Rina A González

Albino H. González Montesinos

Published by Rina A González

Flora, Manny & me

Published by Rina A González

Study and don't fuzz with me!
A Sonnet to Julio

Queens, New York   March 4, 1956

You began it, I'll conclude it.
And with my regained sarcasm
I wonder what I have done;
Why the fuzz? Why such a scandal?

If you write another prose,
While I will be filled with sorrow;
When your hand suffers the blow,
Know that you will be the cause
Of any further arrows.

It would be a rarity that you could win,
The contest of the wits; I am a poet.
Stop the fussing and the daring, dear friend
And let me conquer the muse to my delight
When ever it comes my way.

It is best that you stick to your studies,
Remember that a doctor you will be.
Get rid of all worries and confusions,
That can stop you from prescribing pills to me.

       Published by Rina A González

Manny & I dressed for a school play in 1954

Published by Rina A González

Albino H. González Montesinos

A Dreamer's Heart

Queens, New York   April 3, 1956

I

Oh! Sweet dream how happy you have made me
Bringing peace and joy to this, my lonely heart!
Last night you brought me their sweet memory;
Although it was only a dream, was truly a delight!

II

You know sweet dream, I do so tremble.
Not so much because you are a dream,
But because I know that you're not real.
That is why my poor heart cries
Yet hides the tears of pain
Behind the guise of a gentle sigh.

III

My heart does not belong to me,
For it has sprung, as its buds have blossom.
They are my soul and owners of my heart.
How can I not want to dream of things as awesome?

IV

Yet, we the beggars who believe in dreams,
Whose hearts cry out for our missing essence,
Implore to make our dreams come true,
Before this fleeting illusion vanishes forever and
We are left hoping for a dream that's not to be.

With all my love; to my wife and our children!

    Published by Rina A González

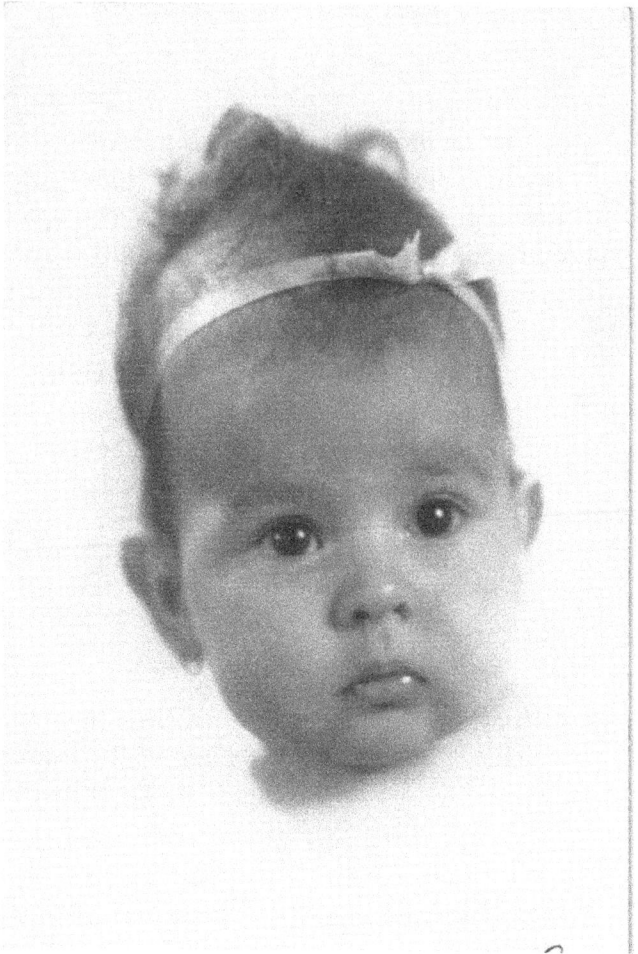

I, {Rina} at 2 months of age

Published by Rina A González

Prepare for destiny's call!
For Rinita

Queens, New York   April 3, 1956

From the dept of your embrace
I see the world through your eyes.
Don't forget to plan ahead
Prepare for destiny's plan.

Get ready for what's to come
Do not fear asking why.
Always give and seek respect
And welcome a guiding hand.

Teachers and divine books
Will always be by your side
For they will open many doors
So you can go on your path.

Trust in what you have learned,
Allow your spirit to soar;
By accepting what life brings,
Life's wonders you will discover.

With love to my daughter Rinita

Published by Rina A González

Published by Rina A González

Albino H. González Montesinos

Unrealistic Heart!
Dialogue with a window

Queens, New York   April 8, 1956

My unrealistic heart!
Look at me, I am a window.
Yet know that I am not a plane.
For that, I would need wings;
And although I am a dreamer
Know that what I am having is a bad dream.

In my desire to see my family
I am rendered useless by my very thoughts.
Obsession is something so unreal
Yet, leads you to believe in what is not.

Like, thinking that I have heard the motor of a plane
Passing over the house while I am sleeping;
When I know that, the airport is too far away
To have its runway run parallel to the bed!

I do not know what is real anymore,
For my unrealistic heart is now possessed.
Now it wants me to believe that my wife is a pilot
And she will be the one to fly the plane.

I look at the clock to see that dawn is near,
Contemplate my unrealistic heart's proclaim.
As I am rendered useless once again;
For how can I in all fairness, evade
Or dare not want this to be the case?

Published by Rina A González

And so the game continues.
I'll be the first to admit that I keep it alive,
For while my illusions are not real
It's nice to think that they will soon be in my arms.

Did you hear that? What could it be I wonder?
It's the engine of a plane
That carries your wife inside....
Be realistic my heart; she has never been a pilot!

Published by Rina A González

Albino H. González Montesinos

As I think of you today
Window and Illusions

Queens, New York   April 8, 1956

Through the window, I see snow
Falling to the earthly plain.
A sigh escape my longing heart,
As I think of you today.

If you see my eyes tear up
Don't confuse them with the rain.
They are coming from my heart
As I think of you again.

Everywhere that I go
I think of having you near.
Yet my delusional mind
Tells me that you are already here.

I've even started to think
That I can fly a darn plane.
And while I try using refrain
It is useless to explain.

How do you tell the mind
That what it wants to obtain
Is difficult at the moment
Because I don't own a plane?

My desire of having you near
Grows deeper with each passing day.
Through the window, I see snow
Falling to the earthly plain.

Published by Rina A González

Our beloved late bother Manny {Manuel}

 Published by Rina A González

To Manuel
A Sonnet

Queens, New York   April 15, 1956

In my home, I have an orchard,
Where my precious flowers grow.
Five children that I adore
Including, my dear son.

Today my dear Manuel
I want to write you this poem,
To clarify that although

Your name is also Garcia
You will not be, like that other
Who forgot to be sincere.

"You will always be our ' King".
You shall triumph and be good looking.
You will be a man of grace,
Who will influence with wisdom
And achieve a higher fame.

After all you are my son;
Manuel González García,
González,
Just like your Pipo.

   Published by Rina A González

My 1st birthday photo with Flora, Mima & Pipo

Published by Rina A González

The Hope of a Memory

Queens, New York   April 22, 1956

Sad memories of those lonely nights
When my life was fading as it shrivel.
My heart does not want to add more pain
That can cause happy memories to drizzle.

While I know that the pass was bittersweet
I rather not remember the details.
By choice, my life took a different course
As a light from above guided my sails.

You cannot hold on to any memory
That is in disagreement with your will.
I feel confident in what I have done.
As the lights that surround me give me skills.

I am happier than I have ever been.
The sunrays unveil a new dawning.
God's eye have shown me an infinite love
That blesses me each day, and every morning.

   Published by Rina A González

La Virgen de la Caridad del Cobre
Cuba's Patron Saint
Our Lady of Charity

Published by Rina A González

Albino H. González Montesinos

To my Beloved Mother!

Queens, New York   April 29, 1956

Today all over the world
The flowers are in full bloom
The air is filled with joy
In celebration of you.

The wind seem to be conspiring
With the mood of this great day
For it fills my heart with love
For the mother of my nave.

No matter if right or wrong
Whether in victory or in failure;
You strive to make us the best
As courageous gladiators.

A mother's love is sublime
And her care is supreme.
She guides us and comforts our souls
By giving us all our dreams.

Oh pure and virtuous mother!
With your constant tender love,
You hold ill towards no one
By teaching us to be strong.

You, like the God above
Forgive all our limitations.
And with your radiant love
Soothe the wound and heal the echoes.

     Published by Rina A González

The petals of these white flowers
Have an everlasting scent.
But none greater than the love
That I know you have for men.

The purity of your soul
Will always be by our side
Guiding us to love all things
As your children, do abide.

You'll always be in our hearts
We sing praises to your name
As the lady that we know
As our beloved embrace.

And although I'm not a poet
My aim is to touch your grace,
By dedicating these words
To your essence and your fame.

Perhaps my muse will be aroused
As I take the pen in hand;
And with words paint you a picture
That will capture your delight.

This poem is for you my Lady,
And to your ever present Rays!

Published by Rina A González

Iris in the Sky
Sonnet

Queen, New York   May 4, 1956

The sky above is adorned
With a lovely tender rainbow
In remembrance of your grace
Charming and good as your glow.

The rainbow blesses the land
By sending rain upon the meadows;
Blessing you and all your charms
As your perfume, the great hallow.

If this verse blushes your cheeks
Please know that it has no malice
My intent is to awaken
The woman inside the goddess.

Rhyming is not a crime;
Nor is the sky or its Rainbow;
Today I dedicate this verse
To you Iris, a woman of many flavors.

Published by Rina A González

Published by Rina A González

Paquita
Sonnet

Queen, New York   May 4, 1956

On Sunday's you go to church
To ask God to bring Fernando.
And as you kneel again ask
To bring your dear Fernando.

You go to church so often
That you have lost the count.
As a friend will tell you gladly;
That the count is one-hundred & eighty nine.

Even though this sonnet is in jest,
It is also to remind you that Fernando
Is also thinking of you, although,
He might not involve The Lord
As often as you do.

The thing is that Fernando will come.
There is no other possible solution.
Between your letters and prayers
Fernando fate has been sealed.

And, if there could be any doubt
That Fernando will soon come,
You will go right back to church and keeling,
Before the Lord, you will place another tune.

   Published by Rina A González

Published by Rina A González

Farewell

Queens, New York   May 13, 1956

Farewell can bring us sadness
As we think how much we'll miss
Those with whom we have shared
Pleasant moments in the spring.

Yet those that leave us today
Are embarking on an adventure.
And our honor is to shed
The light that has been ventured.

Seen that I am also leaving,
Want to say to my colleagues
To never stop learning or growing.
And be ready for what's to be.

And as we face life,
With faith and determination,
We'll show that although we are leaving;
Our teacher's wisdom is present.

His pearls of wisdom his given
He has prepared us by molding,
Like a gardener that has watered
His flowers with love and glory.

And as the days have gone by
You have influenced our minds.
We have learned to trust ourselves
Because of your guiding hand.

            Published by Rina A González

Knowing that now our fate is forged
In the everlasting breath, that binds us.
Today I dedicate this poem,
Knowing that my reasons are sincere.

This farewell is meant for all,
Teacher and students alike.
I cultivate a white rose
For everyone in this class.

Published by Rina A González

Albino H. González Montesinos

For My Country and for Martí

Queens, New York   May 22, 1956

It pains me to see my country
Falling in greater disaster
With her fate yet unknown,
In the absence of her master.

Yet our neighbors rejoice
In our undetermined fate.
My homeland, prophesied by Martí
Is fertile, proud, strong, and brave.

Your sublime, poetic scenes
Are worshiped with a deep passion.
Your politicians can't shine
The dust off those who are called to action.

Those who belicved in Martí
And for whom he was a beacon.
Beacon of the beautiful light
That gave us our truth and freedom.

This man gave us his life.
As a young man was imprisoned,
Was deported; sent to Spain
After was released from prison.

Oh! Cuba who worshiped Martí
His nobility and heroism;
He believed in patriotism,
And gave everything for thee.

   Published by Rina A González

But Cuba – has not followed her cause
And am saddened by the story.
My country is for a few:
Not for all as Martí envisioned.

Because of your doctrine and for thee;
He always fought brilliantly
Until the day that he died
At "Dos Rios" with other proud Cuban Mambíces.

That is why today from here,
Afar from your shores and glory,
I think of my flag and country
And am saddened by the stories.

About Martí, what can I say?
I admire his eloquence and patriotism;
I admire how he dared to dream and for giving
His life to his cause with heroism.

Government: ~ who is in Cuba
Your duty is to love our country.
Don't forget this great man
Who to the world is immortal.

And remember that our homeland
Is the pillar of our braves.
She should not be stepped on by cowards,
Or ruthless pillagers who hate.

Published by Rina A González

Verse from a Greeting Card

Your passion touches my soul
Like a flower touches its gardener.
My lips only need to ask,
For your love; forever after.

Published by Rina A González

Albino H. González Montesinos
1916 ~ 1958

Published by Rina A González

Albino H. González Montesinos

"Desire"

Queens, New York   May 23, 1956

As I read this verse, which found so moving
By the beauty of its words, and by its wisdom,
Know that I would kiss your lips a thousand times.
In love, we are forever after!

Life has imposed this cruel illusion
And because of our separation cannot fulfill
Our truest desires to love and kiss in bliss,
Every morning, every evening; every scheme.

Let us pray to God and to his powers
So that our desires to love do come to pass.
And as our love open the doors of our nature
Never forget that our love was born from two hearts.

The unsigned postcard that I sent you
Much to my astonishment took place
In seeing the beauty of its words
And could only see you, your sweet embrace.

This verse will be remembered
Because of its rhyme and gentle phrase
By two lovers who find passion
Making love looking at each other face to face.

Published by Rina A González

Cover Picture
Photo of our parents when Mima was 14 years old;
along side her faithful companion Beauty

Published by Rina A González

Mima, shopping in downtown Havana.

Published by Rina A González

Our parent's nuptials, December 20, 1941
Havana, Cuba

Published by Rina A González

Romance
Sonnet

Queens, New York   July 15, 1956

Romance! Fragrant and eloquent witness
Of the love that's in my life.
You are my Olympus of love
And the cauldron of my heart.

I have looked for you since childhood
As a sparrow flying high.
You're the dream, I am the dreamer.
I'm the flame; you're the sunlight.

My dreams love and believe
I hold with delight and wonder.
I have fallen for the moon
And her passion is to knight me.

I am a prince who's in love
With the goddess of his heart.
Knowing that dreams do come true.
I am dreaming of your might.

I am romance, you are its touch.
Your the night, I am the day.
You are fire, I am water
And together we make waves.

   Published by Rina A González

Of my life, you are its essence.
Of my heart its tender touch.
Of my mind, its inspiration;
Of my soul, its only love.

Published by Rina A González

For more information on Rina's Literary
Work, please visit her Web Site at:

http://www.angelicgoddesses.com

Thank you!

Rina A González

Published by Rina A González

Published by Rina A González

www.ingramcontent.com/pod-product-compliance
Lightning Source LLC
Chambersburg PA
CBHW060418050426
42449CB00009B/2015